Fifteen Letters
[Khamsata ʿAshara Maktūban]

Fifteen Letters
[Khamsata ʿAshara Maktūban]

SHAIKH ʿABD AL-QĀDIR AL-JĪLĀNĪ
TRANSLATED FROM THE PERSIAN INTO ARABIC
BY ʿALĪ ḤUSĀMU'D-DĪN AL-MUTTAQĪ

AND FROM ARABIC INTO ENGLISH BY MUHTAR HOLLAND

AL-BAZ PUBLISHING, INC.
HOLLYWOOD, FLORIDA

As-Salāmu 'alaikum wa Raḥmatu'llāhi wa Barakātuh. The Greeting of Peace

Cover Design: Rohana Filippi

Using watercolor and wax to combine the beauty of Arabic script with the Qur'ānic message on paper, Italian artist Rohana Filippi has developed her own artistic style through personal research and inner inspiration. Her art is entirely devoted to "expressing Allāh's presence everywhere."
Ms. Filippi, who currently resides in Colombia, has lived and worked in Italy, England, Mexico, and the United States.

Cover Design: Dryden Design, Houston, Texas
Cover Preparation: Susan Lee Graphic Design, Ft. Lauderdale, Florida

Body text set in Jilani and Ghazali fonts by Al-Baz Publishing, Inc.

Printed on acid-free paper.

Second Edition October 2008

Library of Congress
Catalog Card Number: 97–80418

ISBN: 1–882216–16–4
Fifteen Letters

Published by Al-Baz Publishing, Inc.

8771 148th Ave NE, Building C, Redmond, WA 98052
Phone: (425) 891-5444 E-mail: albaz@bellsouth.net

Printed and bound in the United States of America by Sheridan Books, Inc.

Contents

Publisher's Preface

The words of Shaikh 'Abd al-Qādir al-Jīlānī can undoubtedly be considered among the most precious treasures of Islām. Indeed, Al-Baz Publishing was founded with the intention of providing fine English translations of his works for the benefit of English-speaking Muslims everywhere, in the spirit of wishing to share the benefit and blessing we have received ourselves at his hand.

I first became interested in Shaikh 'Abd al-Qādir (may Allah be well pleased with him) in learning from my own spiritual guide and benefactor Bapak Muhammad Sumohadiwidjojo, founder of the Subud brotherhood (may Allāh be well pleased with him), that Allāh had bestowed on the Shaikh the same opening and contact that Bapak himself received from Allāh, and which he has passed on to us.

Anyone familiar with the *latihan kejiwaan* of Subud will know that to be so honored, as Bapak was by Almighty God, is a rare occurrence in the history of mankind, for such grace is usually bestowed on very few of His creatures. My interest thus being aroused, I sought out the surviving manuscripts from their various repositories around the world, and began the task of having them translated. From the very first reading it was apparent to me that what Bapak had said about the Shaikh was true.

O reader! This endeavor is for you! If you find benefit in the reading of these letters, pray that Allāh bless the Shaikh, and pray for us too, that our offering may find acceptance in His sight!

Ruslan Moore
Al-Baz Publishing, Inc.
October, 1997

Acknowledgments

All praise is due to Allāh, the Beneficent, the Merciful!

We bear witness that there is no god except Allāh, and that Muḥammad is the Messenger of Allāh!

Our Lord, thank You for giving us this wholesome task!

Grateful thanks to Muhtar Holland for devoting years of his life to translating these works; may Allāh bless him! Grateful thanks to Omar and Suliman Ghoor, their families and family friends, without whose help the publishing of this volume might have been delayed by years. Thanks also to the many who have helped make this publication possible, among them the following:

Husein Rofé for "Reflections on Subud"

Dr. Hars Kurio of the Staatsbibliothek Preussischer Kulturbesitz, Berlin

Lateef Ismail

Rohana Alkaitis

Liliana Gardner for design fundamentals

Frances Gardner for the flowers

Rohana Filippi for the cover art

Translator's Introduction

This is actually a translation of a translation. Shaikh ʿAbd al-Qādir al-Jīlānī (may Allāh be well pleased with him) wrote these Fifteen Letters in the Persian language, and an Arabic version was produced by someone who describes himself in his Prologue[1] as "this poor beggar, ʿAlī ibn Ḥusāmu 'd-dīn, widely known as al-Muttaqī [the Devout]." I feel a close connection with this colleague of mine, both brotherly and professional, even though he is my senior by more than four hundred years, since he is said to have died in A.H. 977/1569 C.E. In his Prologue, which I beg the reader to consult, he gives an excellent summary description of the nature, style and content of this work.

In one respect, of course, the task of my predecessor was easier than my own. By his reckoning, the Fifteen Letters include approximately two hundred and seventy-five Qurʾānic verses *[āyāt]*. Though I have not seen the Persian text on which al-Muttaqī based his translation, I have no doubt whatsoever that Shaikh ʿAbd al-Qādir (may Allāh be well pleased with him) must have given those Qurʾānic quotations in the original Arabic, assuming that his Muslim reader would be sufficiently familiar with them. In preparing an English translation, I could hardly assume such familiarity on the part of all potential readers, so it was obviously necessary to provide an English rendering, or interpretation, of the many excerpts from the Qurʾān.[2] For the benefit of those who do understand the Arabic, or may wish to study it, a transliteration has also been provided in each instance.

[1] See p. 5 below.

[2] This task has been greatly facilitated by reference to the following invaluable works:
- *The Holy Qurʾān*. Translation and Commentary by Abdullah Yusuf Ali. Leicester, England: The Islamic Foundation, 1975.
- *The Glorious Koran*. English translation by Muhammad Marmaduke Pickthall. London: George Allen and Unwin, 1980.
- Arthur J. Arberry. *The Koran Interpreted*. London: Oxford University Press, 1964.

This English translation is based on a copy of the manuscript numbered WE II 1704,[3] obtained by Al-Baz Publishing from the Staatsbibliothek Preussischer Kulturbesitz in Berlin, Germany. The manuscript itself has no obvious heading, but it has been listed under the title *Ḥikam al-Mawāʿiẓ [Nuggets of Wise Advice]*, an expression used by al-Muttaqī in his Prologue. Another manuscript, presumably of the same work, is listed by the Bodleian Library under the title *Al-Qawl al-Muṣīb fī Taʿrīb al-Makātīb al-Khamsah ʿAshar [Eloquent Arabic Version of the Fifteen Letters]*. The Bodleian also possesses a Persian manuscript, listed under the heading *Maktūbāt [Letters]*, which is described as containing "twenty-five epistles by the famous saint and founder of the Qādirī order...."[4]

In conclusion, let me salute the spirit of al-Muttaqī by echoing his introductory words: "While admitting that I am poorly qualified in the art of expression, especially when it comes to translating from the rich fare provided by the leader of the experts in effective communication [Shaikh ʿAbd al-Qādir al-Jīlānī, may Allāh be well pleased with him], here is the translation I now have to offer.

Muhtar Holland

September 1997

[3] This is the number marked on the photocopy used by the translator. It is presumably more up-to-date than the reference "Berlin 8680," which appears in Brockelmann's *Geschichte der arabischen Literatur*.

[4] The translator had hoped to review these Bodleian manuscripts, but could not obtain access to them before the publication deadline for this edition. If the number "twenty-five" is indeed correct, in the case of the Persian manuscript, it holds out the intriguing prospect of ten additional letters!

Fifteen Letters
[Khamsata ʿAshara Maktūban]

بِسْمِ ٱللَّهِ ٱلرَّحْمَٰنِ ٱلرَّحِيمِ

Allāh's promise is truth. And whose word can be truer than Allāh's?

(Qur'ān 4:122)

Prologue

In the Name of Allāh, the All-Merciful, the All-Compassionate
(and invoking the help that only He can provide!)

Praise be to Allāh, the Lord of All the Worlds, and may Allāh bless our chief, Muḥammad, as well as his family and his companions, each and every one.

Let me now explain the nature of the present work: These are fifteen letters, written by the Imām, the spiritual pole-star of Lordly attributes *[al-quṭb ar-rabbānī]*, the expert teacher *[ustādh]*, the immortal spiritual helper *[al-ghawth aṣ-ṣamadānī]*, the bounteous gift of merciful grace *[al-faiḍ ar-raḥmānī]*, my chieftain and my master, Shaikh Muḥyi'd-dīn ʿAbd al-Qādir al-Ḥasanī al-Jīlānī. May Allāh sanctify his innermost being, and may He enable us to derive benefit from him, from his blessed qualities, and from the blessings of his vast range of knowledge. Āmīn.

Originally written in the Persian language, these letters comprise nuggets of wisdom and spiritual counsel, couched in various forms of allegory, metaphor, paraphrase and quotation, including approximately two hundred and seventy-five Qurʾānic verses. They also contain allusions to the experiences *[adhwāq]* and spiritual states *[ḥālāt]* of the Ṣūfis (may Allāh's good pleasure be conferred upon them all).

An interesting idea presented itself to this poor beggar, ʿAlī ibn Ḥusāmu'd-dīn, widely known as al-Muttaqī [the Devout]. It occurred to me that I might produce an Arabic version, and that I could at least translate the substantial meaning of the text, while admitting that I am poorly qualified in the art of expression, especially when it comes to translating from the rich fare provided by the leader of the experts in effective communication *[āshām imām ahl al-ishāra]*. Here is the translation I now have to offer:

The First Letter

Concerning the initial stage of the attraction exerted by the Truth *[jadhbat al-Ḥaqq]*, and the final stage thereof.

My dear friend!

When the lightning bolts of direct perception *[shuhūd]* come flashing forth from the cloud-bank of the grace of:

Allāh guides to His Light whomever He will. (24:35)	*yahdi 'llāhu li-nūri-hi man yashā'.*

—and the fragrant scents of attainment waft on the wind that blows from the gracious favor of:

He singles out for His mercy whomever He will. (3:74)	*yakhtaṣṣu bi-raḥmati-hi man yashā'.*

—the sweet-smelling plants of intimate friendship will blossom in the meadows of our hearts, and the nightingales of longing will sing in the gardens of our spirits, with the tremulous tones of:

Oh, how I grieve for Joseph! (12:84)	*yā asafā 'alā Yūsuf.*

The fires of yearning will smolder intensely in the stoves of our innermost beings, and the wings of the birds of our thoughts will shed their feathers, from flying too far in the vastness of sublime exaltation.

The stallions of our minds will lose their way in the deserts of intuitive knowledge, the foundations of our intellectual principles will quake from the shock of awe, and the ships of our firm intentions will lose their bearings in the depths of the oceans of:

They did not assign to Allāh the attributes that are due to Him. (6:91)	*wa mā qadaru 'llāha ḥaqqa qadri-hi.*
So it sailed with them in the midst of mountain-like waves. (11:42)	*wa hiya tajrī bi-him fī mawjin ka-'l-jibāl.*

—and at the moment when the waves collide in the ocean of the ardor of:

He loves them and they love Him. (5:54)	*yuḥibbu-hum* *wa yuḥibbūna-hu.*

—each and every one will exclaim, in the spiritual tongue that needs no ordinary words *[lisān al-ḥāl]*:

My Lord, bring me to land in a blessed harbor, for You are the Best of harborers! (23:29)	*Rabbi anzil-nī* *munzalan mubārakan* *wa Anta Khairu 'l-munzilīn.*

So then they will receive, as a foreordained gift, the gracious favor of:

As for those to whom the [reward] most fair has already gone forth from Us.... (21:101)	*inna 'lladhīna* *sabaqat la-hum* *min-na 'l-ḥusnā....*

—and it will bring them ashore on [Mount] Jūdī,[1] a trustworthy landing site *[maqʿad ṣidq]*.[2]

It will introduce them to the sessions of the delirious ecstatics of the Day of:

"Am I not...?" (7:172)	*a-lastu....*

It will spread for them the table-mat of the bounty of:

To those who do good belongs the finest—and an extra reward! (10:26)	*li'lladhīna aḥsanu 'l-ḥusnā* *wa ziyāda.*

—and it will pass to them the cups of attainment, filled from the jugs of nearness, by the hands of the cupbearers of:

And their Lord will quench their thirst with a pure drink. (76:21)	*wa saqā-hum Rabbu-hum* *sharāban ṭahūrā.*

They will thus be honored with the everlasting estate and the endlessly enduring fortune of:

And when you see, there you will see a state of bliss and a great domain. (76:20)	*wa idhā raʾaita* *thamma raʾaita* *naʿīman wa mulkan kabīrā.*

The Second Letter

Concerning the significance of dedicated striving *[mujāhada]* and spiritual training *[riyāḍa]*, and the fruits thereof.

My dear friend!

You must place the ingot of your quest inside the crucible of:

And as for those who strive for the sake of Our cause.... (29:69)	*wa 'llādhīna jāhadū fī-nā....*

—and refine it with the fire of:

And Allāh warns you to beware of Himself. (3:30)	*wa yuḥadhdhiru-kumu 'llāhu Nafsa-h.*

It will thus become purged of sin, to the point where it befits the coin of:

We surely guide them in Our ways. (29:69)	*la-nahdiyanna-hum subula-nā.*

—and its worth and value will increase in the market of:

Allāh has bought from the believers their persons and their goods, the Garden [of Paradise] being theirs for the price. (9:111)	*inna 'llāha 'shtarā mina 'l-mu'minīna anfusa-hum wa amwāla-hum bi-anna la-humu 'l-janna.*

You must treat this as your capital investment, in order to acquire the merchandise of:

Surely pure religion is only for Allāh. (39:3)	*a-lā li'llahi 'd-dīnu 'l-khāliṣ.*

—and so that a clue to the secrets of:

Those who are sincerely devoted are in possession of a mighty fortune.[3]	*wa 'l-mukhliṣūna ʿalā ḥaẓẓin ʿaẓīm.*

—may be decoded for you, and so that rays from the lights of:

Is he whose breast Allāh has expanded to receive Islām, so that he is guided by a light from his Lord…? (39:22)	*a-fa-man sharaḥa 'llāhu ṣadra-hu li'l-islāmi fa-huwa ʿalā nūrin min Rabbi-h.*

—may shine in your presence. For then, in your heart, you will feel the stimulating impact of the invitation:

Call upon Me and I will answer you. (40:60)	*udʿū-nī astajib la-kum.*

—and you will ascend from the low-lying hollow of:

Say: "The enjoyment of this world is of little value." (4:77)	*qul matāʿu 'd-dunyā qalīl.*

—to the mountain peak of:

But the Hereafter is better and more lasting. (87:17)	*wa 'l-ākhiratu khairun wa abqā.*

You will inhale a refreshing aroma from the breeze of the nearness of:

And We are nearer to him [than the jugular vein] (50:16)	*wa Naḥnu aqrabu ilai-hi [min ḥabli 'l-warīd].*

The tree of your heart will be shaken by that breeze, and you will take refuge from all others [apart from Allāh] in the autumn gales of:

Say "Allāh!," then leave them [to their idle prattling]. (6:91)	*quli 'llāhu thumma dhar-hum [fī khawḍi-him yalʿabūn].*

—in the orchard of the contemplation of:

So do not call upon another god, together with Allāh. (28:88) [4]	*wa lā tadʿu maʿa 'llāhi ilāhan ākhar.*

The winds of the springtime of:

But as for those to whom the reward most fair has already gone forth from Us, [they shall be kept far from it (from Hell)]. (21:101)	*inna 'lladhīna sabaqat la-hum min-na 'l-ḥusnā: [ulāʾika ʿan-hā mubʿadūn].*

—will blow upon you, and the fleecy clouds *[yaʿālīl]* of gracious favor and the dense clouds *[saḥāʾib]* of:

Allāh chooses for Himself whomever He will. (42:13)	*Allāhu yajtabī ilai-hi man yashāʾu.*

—will shower upon you the raindrops of copious abundance.

The ground of the meadows of the heart will thus become verdant with the plants of:

And We had taught him knowledge from Our presence. (18:65)	*wa ʿallamnā-hu* *min ladun-nā ʿilmā.*

—and the trees of the orchards of the spirit will be laden with the fruits of:

The mercy of Allāh is close indeed to those who do good. (7:56)	*inna raḥmata 'llāhi* *qarībun mina 'l-muḥsinīn.*

—and the springs of attainment will flow in the valleys of the innermost being, from the source of:

A fountain at which those brought near [to the Lord] do drink. (83:28)	*ʿainan yashrabu* *bi-ha 'l-muqarrabūn.*

The herald of the good fortune of:

Such is the bounty of Allāh, which He bestows on whom He will. (62:4)	*dhālika faḍlu 'llāhi* *yuʾtī-hi man yashāʾ.*

—will cheer you with the good news of:

Do not fear and do not grieve, but hear good tidings of the Garden [of Paradise] that you have been promised. (41:30)	*al-lā takhāfū wa lā taḥzanū* *wa abshirū bi'l-jannati 'llatī* *kuntum tūʿadūn.*

—and Riḍwān, the keeper of the blissful Garden of:

Allāh is well pleased with them, and they are well pleased with Him. (98:8)[5]	*raḍiya 'llāhu ʿan-hum* *wa raḍū ʿan-h.*

—will proclaim the invitation:

Eat and drink, with wholesome appetite, as reward for the work you used to do. (52:19)	*kulū wa 'shrabū* *hanīʾan bi-mā* *kuntum taʿmalūn.*

The Third Letter

Concerning fear and hope, and the fruits thereof.

My dear friend!

Be afraid of a day when a man will flee from his brother, from his mother and his father, from his consort and his children. Reflect on the reckoning of:

And whether you publish what is inside yourselves, or keep it hidden, Allāh will call you to account for it. (2:284)	*wa in tubdū mā fī anfusi-kum aw tukhfū-hu yuḥāsib-kum bi-hi 'llāh.*

Do not concern yourself with the fortunes of:

Those, they are like cattle. (7:179)	*ulā'ika ka-'l-an'āmi.*

Lower your head in the contemplation of:

So remember Me, and I will remember you. (2:152)	*fa-'dhkurū-nī adhkur-kum.*

Open the eye of your heart in the witnessing of:

That day will faces be resplendent, looking toward their Lord. (75:22,23)	*wujūhun yawma'idhin nāḍira : ilā Rabbi-hā nāẓira.*

—and recollect some of the bliss of:

There you will have all that your souls desire, and there you will have all that you pray for. (41:31)	*wa la-kum fī-hā mā tashtahī anfusu-kum wa la-kum fī-hā mā tadda'ūn.*

Then maybe you will hear, with the ear of your heart, the call of the crier of:

And Allāh summons to the Abode of Peace. (10:25)	*wa 'llāhu yad'ū ilā dāri 's-salām.*

—and wake up from the sleep of the heedlessness of:

The life of this world is nothing but a sport and a pastime. (47:36)	*inna-ma 'l-ḥayātu 'd-dunyā la'ibun wa lahw.*

—and stride forth, on the foot of your head, in pursuit of the degrees of:

And the frontrunners, the frontrunners: those will be the ones brought near, in the Gardens of Delight. (56:10–12)	*wa 's-sābiqūna 's-sābiqūn: ulā'ika 'l-muqarrabūn: fī jannāti 'n-na'īm.*

—and strike the racehorse of your aspiration with the whip of your firm resolve.

Then maybe the harbinger of the tender kindnesses of:

Allāh is Ever-Gentle to His servants. (42:19)	*Allāhu Laṭīfun bi-'ibādi-hi.*

—will come to meet you, with trays containing the presents of:

For them there are good tidings. (10:64)	*la-humu 'l-bushrā.*

—and you will triumph, with reinforcement from the armies of:

And to Allāh belong the hosts of the heavens and the earth. (48:4)[6]	*wa li'llāhi junūdu 's-samāwāti wa 'l-arḍ.*

—over the hostile forces of:

Surely Satan is to the human being an obvious enemy. (12:5)	*inna 'sh-shaiṭāna li'l-insāni 'aduwwun mubīn.*

You will escape from the snare of the passion of:

Surely the self is always inciting to evil. (12:53)	*inna 'n-nafsa la-ammāratun bi's-sū'i.*

—and then the imprints of the tender mercies of the secrets of:

Observe your duty to Allāh, and Allāh will teach you. (2:282)	*wa 'ttaqu 'llāh: wa yu'allimu-kumu 'llāh.*

—will appear on the tablet of your heart.

The bird of your spirit *[rūḥ]* will remember the groves of Paradise *[ḥaẓā'ir al-quds]*. It will soar into the vast space of:

And follow the ways of your Lord, [which are] smooth to travel. (16:69)	*fa-'slukī subula Rabbi-ki dhululā.*

—on the wing of ardent longing, and you will gather some of the fruits of intimate friendship *[uns]* in the orchards of:

[Then] eat of all the fruits. (16:69)	*[thumma] kulī min kulli 'th-thamarāti.*

The mirror of your innermost being *[sirr]* will reflect the luminous rays of the [divine] manifestations *[tajalliyāt]*, so that you are allowed to discover the secret of:

You cause the night to pass into the day. (3:27)[7]	*tūliju 'l-laila* *fi 'n-nahāri.*

The garden of your heart will soon be made verdant by the showering rains of the mercies of:

And down from the sky We have sent blessed water, and so produced gardens and the grain of crops. (50:9)	*wa nazzalnā mina 's-samā'i* *mā'an mubārakan fa-anbatnā bi-hi* *jannātin wa ḥabba 'l-ḥaṣīd.*

—and so the whole of it will come to be like the garden of Iram.[8] You will understand the enigmatic indications of:

And [thereby] We revived a land that was dead. (50:11)	*wa aḥyainā [bi-hi]* *baldatan maitā:*

—and removed from your eyes will be the curtains of:

But now We have removed from you your covering, and so today your sight is piercing. (50:22)	*fa-kashafnā 'an-ka* *ghiṭā'a-ka* *fa-baṣaru-ka 'l-yawma ḥadīd.*

You will thus become immersed in the perfection of direct experience *[mushāhada]*. There will be a time when you plunge deep into the ocean of the independence *[istighnā']* of:

Allāh is indeed Independent of all the worlds. (3:97)	*inna 'llāha Ghaniyyun* *'ani 'l-'ālamīn.*

There will be a time when you stagger in bewilderment, caught in the sandstorm *[samūm]* of the awe-inspiring impact of:

Do they then feel secure against Allāh's devising? (7:99)	*a-fa-aminū* *makra 'llāh.*

There will also be a time when ardent yearning sets you singing like the nightingale *['andalīb]* in the orchard of glorification *[tamjīd]*, in tune with the gentle breeze of:

And do not despair of the Spirit of Allāh. (12:87)	*wa lā tai'asū* *min Rawḥi 'llāh.*

Moved by the raptures of ecstasy *[ghalabāt al-wajd]*, you will then raise your voice in the joyful delight of:

I do indeed detect the scent of Joseph. (12:94)	*innī la-ajidu* *rīḥa Yūsufa.*

—so the envious will say, with the tongue of blame:

By Allāh, you are surely in your ancient error. (12:95)	*ta'llāhi inna-ka* *la-fī ḍalāli-ka 'l-qadīm.*

—but when they see the effect of:

He laid it on his face, and he became able to see again. (12:96)	*alqā-hu ʿalā wajhi-hi* *fa-'rtadda baṣīrā.*

—they will plead with you, in pathetic and humble entreaty, to:

Ask forgiveness of our sins on our behalf, for we have certainly been guilty. (12:97)	*[i]staghfir la-nā* *dhunūba-nā* *innā kunnā khāṭiʾīn.*

—and they will say, from a feeling of honesty *[ṣidq]* and sincerity *[ikhlāṣ]*:

Allāh has indeed preferred you over us. (12:91)	*la-qad āthara-ka 'llāhu* *ʿalai-nā.*

—and you will say, in the stations of intimate converse *[munājāt]*:

O my Lord, You have given me some sovereignty, and You have taught me something of the interpretation of tales. O Creator of the heavens and the earth, You are my Protecting Friend in this world and the hereafter. Let me die as one who is truly submissive [to You], and join me with the righteous. (12:101)	*Rabbi qad ātaita-nī* *mina 'l-mulki* *wa ʿallamta-nī* *min taʾwīli 'l-aḥādīth:* *Fāṭira 's-samāwāti* *wa 'l-arḍ:* *Anta Waliyyī fi 'd-dunyā* *wa 'l-ākhira:* *tawaffa-nī musliman* *wa alḥiq-nī bi'ṣ-ṣāliḥīn.*

The Fourth Letter

Concerning the urgent need to banish heedlessness, and turn in repentance from sinful acts of disobedience.

My dear friend!

Heedlessness and vain indulgence in the life of this world are not among the tokens of felicity. Do you not hear, with the ear of your heart, the posing of the question:

Are you content with the life of this world, rather than that of the Hereafter? (9:38)	*a-raḍītum bi-'l-ḥayāti 'd-dunyā mina 'l-ākhira.*

Are you not frightened by the threat:

If someone is blind in this world, he will also be blind in the hereafter, and even further astray from the road. (17:72) ?	*wa man kāna fī hādhihi aʿmā fa-huwa fī 'l-ākhirati aʿmā wa aḍallu sabīlā.*

Do you not contemplate the menace:

Their reckoning has drawn near to mankind, while they are still turning away in heedlessness. (21:1) ?	*iqtaraba li'n-nāsi ḥisābu-hum wa hum fī ghaflatin muʿriḍūn.*

Do you not pay attention to the reprimand:

Whoever desires the harvest of this world, We shall give him some of it, but in the hereafter he will have no share. (42:20) ?	*wa man kāna yurīdu ḥartha 'd-dunyā nu'ti-hi min-hā wa mā la-hu fī 'l-ākhirati min naṣīb.*

Do you not take notice of the admonition:

Then, as for him who was insolent and preferred the life of this world, surely Hell shall be his home. (79:37–39) ?	*fa-ammā man ṭaghā wa āthara 'l-ḥayāta 'd-dunyā fa-inna 'l-jaḥīma hiya 'l-ma'wā.*

How long will you wander in the desert of heedless neglect? How long will you stay shackled by the chains of passionate desire? You must enter the hermit's cell *[ṣawmaʿa]* of:

Repent unto Allāh. (24:31)	*tūbū ila 'llāhi.*

—and turn, in that state of present awareness, to face the prayer-niche *[miḥrāb]* of:

And turn to your Lord in repentance. (39:54)	*wa anībū* *ilā Rabbi-kum.*

—and say, with the tongue of truthfulness *[ṣidq]* and sincere devotion *[ikhlāṣ]*:

I have turned my face toward Him who created the heavens and the earth, as a *Ḥanīf*; I am not one of those who attribute partners [to Allāh]. (6:79)	*innī wajjahtu wajhiya li'llādhī* *faṭara 's-samāwāti wa 'l-arḍa* *ḥanīfan wa mā ana* *mina 'l-mushrikīn.*

You may then be allowed to discover the priceless gems of the secrets of:

And He it is who accepts repentance from His servants, and pardons evil deeds. (42:25)	wa *Huwa 'lladhī* *yaqbalu 't-tawbata ʿan ʿibādi-hi* *wa yaʿfū ʿani 's-sayyiʾāti.*

—from the treasure houses of the tender mercies of:

Allāh is indeed All-Forgiving, All-Compassionate. (2:199)	*inna 'llāha Ghafūrun* *Raḥīm.*

—and you may be greeted with good tidings by the courier of the providential favor of:

Truly Allāh loves those who turn to Him repentant, and He loves those who keep themselves in purity. (2:222)	*inna 'llāha* *yuḥibbu 't-tawwābīna* *wa yuḥibbu 'l-mutaṭahhirīn.*

You will then set out to travel the roads of:

And You exalt whom You will. (3:26)	*wa tuʿizzu man tashāʾu.*

—and the herald of good fortune will call out to you, in the spiritual language that needs no ordinary words *[bi-lisāni 'l-ḥāl]*:

Those who say: "Our Lord is Allāh," and then travel straight, no fear shall be upon them, nor shall they grieve. (46:13)	*inna 'lladhīna qālū Rabbu-na 'llāhu* *thumma 'staqāmū* *fa-lā khawfun ʿalai-him* *wa lā hum yaḥzanūn.*

The Fifth Letter

Concerning the significance of the immediate presence *[maʿiyya]* of Allāh (Exalted is He), and the fact that His knowledge (Exalted is He) embraces all things.

My dear friend!

When the suns of our spiritual experiences *[maʿārif]* rise from their points of ascension in the skies of our innermost beings, the earths of our hearts will be illumined by the light of:

And the earth will shine with the light of its Lord. (39:69)	*wa ashraqati 'l-arḍu bi-nūri Rabbi-hā.*

—and the coverings of the darkness of ignorance will be removed from the eyes of our minds, with the ointment of:

But now We have removed from you your covering. (50:22)	*fa-kashafnā ʿan-ka ghiṭāʾa-ka.*

The eyes of our inward intellects will then be dazzled by the radiant emanations of the lights of holiness *[al-quds]*. Our processes of thought will wonder in amazement, at the disclosure of the marvelous secrets of the realm of the spiritual kingdom *[al-malakūt]*.

Excited by the thrill of ardent love *[al-ʿishq]*, the seeker will go a-wandering in the deserts of the quest. Then, in the sites of nearness, the raptures of yearning *[ghalabāt ash-shawq]* will become familiar to him, and the herald of:

Allāh is truly Bountiful toward mankind. (10:60)	*inna 'llāha la-Dhū Faḍlin ʿala 'n-nāsi.*

—will proclaim:

And He is with you wherever you may be. (57:4)	*wa Huwa maʿa-kum aina-mā kuntum.*

Once he has discovered the secret of 'togetherness' *[al-maʿiyya]*, the seeker will lose his personal existence, in compliance with the dictate of:

And do not set together with Allāh another god. (51:51)	*wa lā taj'alū ma'a 'llāhi ilāhan ākhar.*

As soon as he has plunged into the sea of the personal extinction *[fanā']* of:

No part of the matter is your concern. (3:128)	*laisa la-ka mina 'l-amri shai'un.*

—so that he may obtain the jewel of the affirmation of Oneness *[tawḥīd]*, the waves of solicitude *[ghaira]* will fling him into the ocean of sublimity *['aẓama]*. Each time he makes for the shore, in the plight of bewilderment, he must say:

My Lord, I have wronged myself, so forgive me! (28:16)	*Rabbi innī ẓalamtu nafsī fa-'ghfir lī.*

—for then he will be picked up by the rescue vessels of the kind favors of:

And We have carried them on land and sea. (17:70)	*wa ḥamalnā-hum fi 'l-barri wa 'l-baḥri.*

—and they will set him down on the beach of the the tender kindness of:

We visit with Our mercy whom We will. (12:56)	*nuṣību bi-raḥmati-nā man nashā'u.*

They will hand him the keys to the treasure houses of the mysteries of:

And Allāh is always encompassing all things. (4:126)	*wa kāna 'llāhu bi-kulli shai'in Muḥīṭā.*

—and they will point out to him the indications of:

And that unto your Lord is the final destination. (53:42)	*wa anna ilā Rabbi-ka 'l-muntahā.*

He will thereby come to know the meaning of:

And He revealed to His servant that which He revealed. (53:10)	*fa-awḥā ilā 'abdi-hi mā awḥā.*

—and he will understand the implication of:

Indeed, he saw one of the greatest signs of his Lord. (53:18)	*la-qad ra'ā min āyāti Rabbi-hi 'l-kubrā.*

The Sixth Letter

Concerning (1) the significance of the all-compelling nature *[qahhāriyya]* of the attraction *[jadhba]* exerted by the Lord of Truth (Exalted is He), (2) compliance therewith on the part of the rebellious forces of self-will *[nafsāniyya]*, and (3) the occurrence of the resurrection of the spiritual traveler *[qiyāmat 'l-sālik]* in this world.

My dear friend!

When the armies of the providential ecstasies *[jadhabāt]* of:

Allāh chooses for Himself whomever He will. (42:13)	*Allāhu yajtabī ilai-hi man yashā'u.*

—have conquered the government of our hearts, they will humble and exercise the arrogant aspirations of our domineering selves *[an-nufūs al-ammāra]* with the bridles of the training of:

And strive for Allāh's sake with all the effort He deserves. (22:78)	*wa jāhidū fi 'llāhi ḥaqqa jihādi-h.*

They will confine the tyrants of passion inside the prison of dutiful devotion *[taqwā]*, bound in the chains of strenuous exertion *[mujāhada]*, and they will shackle the Pharaohs of desire with the fetters of:

Obey Allāh and obey the Messenger. (4:59)[9]	*aṭī'u 'llāha wa aṭī'u 'r-rasūla.*

They will chastise the agents of our wishes and our preferences with the discipline of:

He who does wrong will have the recompense thereof. (4:123)	*man ya'mal sū'an yujza bi-hi.*

They will completely demolish the innovations that constitute our conventional habits and customary practices, along with the foundations that support the pillars of fraud and deception. The herald of the spiritual state *[munādi 'l-ḥāl]* will proclaim, in the language of veracity *[lisān aṣ-ṣidq]:*

Kings, when they enter a township, ruin it and make the noblest of its people the lowest. (27:34)	*inna 'l-mulūka idhā dakhalū* *qaryatan afsadū-hā wa ja'alū* *a'izzata ahli-hā adhilla.*

The courtyard of our hearts will thus be purified and cleansed of the stain made by the filthy refuse of the house of:

If anyone desires anything other than Islām as a religion, it will never be accepted of him. (3:85)	*wa man yabtaghi* *ghaira 'l-islāmi dīnan* *fa-lan yuqbala min-h.*

—the gardens of our spirits will acquire a fragrance from the breezes of the gracious favors of:

He whom Allāh guides, he is indeed the one who is guided aright. (7:178)	*man yahdi 'llāhu* *fa-huwa 'l-muhtadī.*

—the surfaces of the leaves of our innermost beings will be engraved with the calligraphic markings of the subtleties of:

As for such, He has written faith upon their hearts. (58:22)	*ulā'ika kataba* *fī qulūbi-himu 'l-īmāna.*

—and the lamp of our consciences will become the mirror of the lightning bolts of direct vision, through the shining rays of the lights of:

And Allāh will perfect His light. (61:8)	*wa 'llāhu mutimmu nūri-hi.*

The spiritual state of the seeker will then fit the description of how it is to be:

On the day when the earth will be changed to other than this earth. (14:48)[10]	*yawma* *tubaddalu 'l-arḍu* *ghaira 'l-arḍi.*

The seemingly unshakable mountains of his ardent yearnings will disintegrate into scattered particles of dust *[haba'an manthūrā]*,[11] and he will say with the tongue of truthfulness:

And you will see the mountains, which you suppose to be solidly fixed, flying by with the flight of clouds. (27:88)	*wa tarā 'l-jibāla* *taḥsabu-hā jāmidatan* *wa hiya tamurru* *marra 's-saḥāb.*

The Isrāfīl[12] of intense love *[ʿishq]* will blow the trumpet of:

And the Trumpet will be blown. (39:68)	*wa nufikha* *fi 'ṣ-ṣūri.*

—until there is no longer any mystery about the stunning cause of:

So whoever is in the heavens and whoever is in the earth will swoon away. (39:68)	*fa-ṣaʿiqa* *man fi 's-samāwāti* *wa man fi 'l-arḍi.*

Then, just in time, the announcer of the good fortune of:

The greatest terror will not grieve them.[13] (21:103)	*lā yaḥzunu-* *humu 'l-fazaʿu 'l-akbaru.*

—will arrive to reinvigorate them. He will summon them to the highest heaven *[ʿIlliyyūn]*,[14] a sure abode *[maqʿad ṣidq]*.[15] As he delivers the glad tidings of:

Good news for you this day. (57:12)[16]	*bushrā-kumu 'l-yawma.*

—he will open for them the gates of the Gardens of Delight, and he will say:

Peace be upon you. Well you have fared, so enter in, to dwell therein forever. (39:73)	*salāmun ʿalai-kum* *ṭibtum* *fa-'dkhulū-hā khālidīn.*

—and they will say:

Praise be to Allāh, who has fulfilled His promise to us, and has caused us to inherit the land, for us to make our dwelling wherever we will in the Garden [of Paradise]. How splendid is the wage of those who labor! (39:74)	*al-ḥamdu li'llāhi 'lladhī* *ṣadaqa-nā waʿda-hu* *wa awratha-nā 'l-arḍa* *natabawwaʾu min al-jannati* *ḥaithu nashāʾ:* *fa-niʿma ajru al-ʿāmilīn.*

The Seventh Letter

Concerning pious abstinence *[zuhd]* and the fruits thereof.

My dear friend!

You must pass beyond the realm of the delusion *[ghurūr]* of:

So do not let the life of this world delude you, and do not let the Deceiver deceive you in regard to Allāh. (31:33)	*fa-lā taghurranna-* *kumu 'l-ḥayātu 'd-dunyā:* *wa lā yaghurranna-kum* *bi-'llāhi 'l-Gharūr.*

—and remember the stations of the people in whose presence *[ḥuḍūr]*:

[You will recognize] in their faces the cheerful radiance of bliss. (83:24)	*[taʿrifu] fī wujūhi-him* *naḍrata 'n-naʿīm.*

Then maybe you will sniff, with the nostrils of your heart, a fragrant aroma from the scents of the orchard of:

Then there will be comfort and joy, and a Garden of Delight. (56:89)	*fa-rawḥun wa raiḥānun* *wa jannatu naʿīm.*

—and drink a draught from the cup of:

They are given to drink of a pure wine, sealed, the seal of which is musk. (83:25,26)	*yusqawna min raḥīqin* *makhtūm:* *khitāmu-hu misk.*

—and have disclosed to you the subtle details of the secrets of:

The truth has surely come to you from your Lord. (10:94)	*la-qad jāʾa-ka 'l-ḥaqqu* *min Rabbi-ka.*

While you rest on the carpet of the strict observance of:

And do not call, apart from Allāh, on that which can neither profit you nor hurt you. (10:106)	*wa lā tadʿu min dūni 'llāhi* *mā lā yanfaʿu-ka* *wa lā yaḍurru-k.*

—you will hear, from the late-night entertainer *[musāmir]* of the intimate friendship *[uns]* of:

We shall relate to you the finest of stories. (12:3)	*Naḥnu naquṣṣu ʿalai-ka aḥsana 'l-qaṣaṣi.*

—the tale told by night of:

Both a witness and that to which witness is borne. (85:3)	*wa shāhidin wa mashhūd.*

There will be a time, therefore, when you are thrilled with the utmost delight, as you savor the melodious tones of the declaration:

So give good tidings to My servants who listen to advice, and then follow the best of it. (39:17,18)	*fa-bashshir ʿibād: alladhīna yastamiʿūna 'l-qawla fa-yattabiʿūna aḥsana-h.*

There will be a point at which you lower your head in sorrowful contemplation, in response to the shocks of the awe-inspiring impact of:

So keep to the straight path, as you have been commanded, and those who repent along with you. (11:112)	*fa-'staqim ka-mā umirta wa man tāba maʿa-ka.*

There will be a moment when you cling tightly to the firm rope of:

And hold fast, all of you together, to the lifeline of Allāh. (3:103)	*wa 'ʿtaṣimū bi-ḥabli 'llāhi jamīʿan.*

There will be a moment when you hang on to the peg of:

And help comes only from the presence of Allāh. (3:126)[17]	*wa ma 'n-naṣru illā min ʿindi 'llāhi.*

There will be a time when you are submerged in the frightful ocean of:

We shall draw them on little by little, without their knowing from where. (7:182) [18]	*sa-nastadriju-hum min ḥaithu lā yaʿlamūn.*

—and a point when you land safely on the shore of:

To you, Allāh is surely Ever-Gentle, All-Compassionate. (57:9)	*inna 'llāha bi-kum la-Raʾūfun Raḥīm.*

You will then gather from the gardens of:

Whoever hopes to meet his Lord... (18:110)	*fa-man kāna yarjū liqāʾa Rabbi-hi...*

—the fruits of:

> So let him do righteous work. (18:110) *fa-l'-ya'mal 'amalan ṣāliḥan.*

You will scoop fresh water, with the hands of sincere devotion *[ikhlāṣ]*, from the streams of:

For all there will be degrees, according to what they have done. (6:132)	*wa li-kullin darajātun mim-mā 'amilū.*

—and in the shade of the lotus tree *[sidra]* of:

My prayer, my ritual sacrifice, my living and my dying are for Allāh, the Lord of All the worlds. (6:162)	*inna ṣalātī wa nusukī wa maḥyā-ya wa mamātī li'llāhi Rabbi 'l-'ālamīn.*

—you will relish the food from the table of the blissful joy of:

And who fulfills his covenant more truly than Allāh? So rejoice! (9:111)	*wa man awfā bi-'ahdi-hi mina 'llāhi fa-'stabshirū.*

—and from the herald of gracious favor you will hear the proclamation:

O My servants, for you there is no fear this Day, and you are not the ones who will be feeling sad. (43:68)	*yā 'ibādi lā khawfun 'alai-kumu 'l-yawma wa lā antum taḥzanūn.*

The Eighth Letter

Concerning intimate friendship *[uns]* and the fruits thereof.

My dear friend!

When a sweet sound from the captain of intimate friendship *[uns]* reaches the ears of our hearts, they will savor delightful memories of listening to the melodious tones of the pronouncement:

"Am I not your Lord?" (7:172)	*a-lastu bi Rabbi-kum.*

—and they will recall the delirious raptures *[sakarāt]* of the spiritual states they experienced when:

They said: "Yes indeed, [we testify]." (7:172)	*qālū* *balā [shahidnā].*

The nightingales of sorrows will trill with the chords of the lovely melody of:

Oh, how I grieve for Joseph! (12:84)	*yā asafā ʿalā Yūsuf.*

The lute of the cherubs *[ʿūd al-karūb]* will resonate with the echo of the heartbreak of:

And his eyes turned white with sorrow, for he was suppressing his anguish. (12:84)	*wa 'byaḍḍat ʿainā-hu* *mina 'l-ḥuzni* *fa-huwa kaẓīm.*

The mandolin *[ṭunbūr]* of separation will vibrate with the sound of:

Only unto Allāh do I complain of my grief and my sorrow. (12:86)	*inna-mā ashkū* *baththī wa ḥuznī ila 'llāhi.*

—to the rhythm of:

But come, sweet patience! (12:18)	*fa-ṣabrun jamīl.*

The lightning flashes of the ecstasies *[jadhabāt]* of ardent yearning will gleam in the vastness of the skies of our innermost beings, with the radiance of:

The brilliance of His lightning all but snatches away the sight. (24:43)	*yakādu sanā barqi-hi* *yadhhabu bi'l-abṣār.*

—to the point where the eyes of our mental faculties are obliterated, and tears of grief drop from the clouds of the eyes of our spirits *[arwāḥ]*, so that the fields of the farm of:

If someone desires the harvest of the hereafter, We shall give him an increase in his harvest. (42:20)	*man kān yurīdu* *ḥartha al-ākhirati* *nazid la-hu fī ḥarthi-h.*

—become verdant with the plants of:

Allāh has promised you many spoils of booty. (48:20)	*wa'ada-kumu 'llāhu* *maghānima kathīratan.*

—and the gardens sown with the hopes of:

And whoever puts all his trust in Allāh, He will suffice him. (65:3)	*wa man yatawakkal 'ala 'llāhi* *fa-Huwa ḥasbu-h.*

—become fragrant with the aromatic perfumes of:

Allāh surely attains His purpose. (65:3)	*inna 'llāha bālighu amri-h.*

—entirely and completely, while the branches of the trees of patience *[ṣabr]* bear the fruits of:

Those who patiently persevere will truly receive a reward without measure. (39:10)	*innamā yuwaffa 'ṣ-ṣābirūna* *ajra-hum* *bi-ghairi ḥisāb.*

—to the fullest extent of perfection, and the winds that blow are the winds that carry the providential bounty of:

This is Our gift, so bestow or withhold [without reckoning]. (38:39)	*hādhā 'aṭā'u-nā fa-'mnun* *aw amsik [bi-ghairi ḥisāb].*

—and the herald of:

And your Lord is the All-Forgiving, the One who is Full of Mercy. (18:58)	*wa Rabbu-ka 'l-Ghafūru* *Dhu 'r-Raḥma.*

—proclaims:

This is indeed Our provision, which can never waste away. (38:54)	*inna hādhā la-rizqu-nā* *mā la-hu min nafād.*

The Ninth Letter

Concerning the incentive to seek the companionship of the righteous *[ṣuḥbat al-abrār]* and the fruits thereof, and to practice abstinence *[zuhd]* from this world.

My dear friend!

You must turn aside from the tempting urges of carnal appetites:

And follow not desire, lest it lead you astray from Allāh's path. (38:26)	*wa lā tattabiʿi 'l-hawā* *fa-yuḍilla-ka ʿan sabīli 'llāh.*

—and depart from the dwellings of heedless neglect:

And do not obey someone whose heart We have made heedless of Our remembrance. (18:28)	*wa lā tuṭiʿ* *man aghfalnā qalba-hu* *ʿan dhikri-nā.*

—and shun the companionship of hard-hearted folk:

But woe unto those whose hearts are hardened against the remembrance of Allāh. (39:22)	*fa-wailun li'l-qāsiyati* *qulūbu-hum* *min dhikri 'llāh.*

You must hear, with the ears of your heart, from the summoner of:

Respond to your Lord, before there comes a day from Allāh that cannot be turned back. (42:47)	*istajībū li-Rabbi-kum* *min qabli an yaʾtiya yawmun* *lā maradda la-hu mina 'llāh.*

—the summons of:

Is not the time now ripe for the hearts of those who believe to be humbled to the Remembrance of Allāh? (57:16)	*a-lam yaʾni li'lladhīna āmanū* *an takhshaʿa qulūbu-hum* *li-dhikri 'llāhi.*

You must wake up from the sleep of delusion:

And do not let the Deceiver deceive you in regard to Allāh. (31:33)	*wa lā yaghurranna-kum* *bi-'llāhi 'l-Gharūr.*

—in response to the admonition:

What, does man suppose that he will be left to wander aimlessly? (75:36)	*a-yaḥsabu 'l-insānu an yutraka sudā.*

You must inquire about the stations of the people of present awareness:

Men whom neither commerce nor trafficking diverts from the remembrance of Allāh. (24:37)	*rijālun lā tulhī-him tijāratun wa lā bai'un 'an dhikri 'llāhi.*

You must journey toward the Ka'ba of the intended destination, on the foot of the head, in the desert of the dedication of:

And devote yourself to Him with intense devotion. (73:8)	*wa tabattal ilai-hi tabtīlā.*

—with the traveling provision of:

Say "Allāh!," then leave them [to their idle prattling]. (6:91)	*quli 'llāhu thumma dhar-hum [fī khawḍi-him yal'abūn].*

—and on the riding camel of the commitment of:

And I commit my affair to Allāh. (40:44)	*wa ufawwiḍu amrī ila 'llāh.*

—with the caravan of the truthful people of:

And be with the faithful. (9:119)	*wa kūnū ma'a 'ṣ-ṣādiqīn.*

You must pass beyond the dwellings of the vanities of the world of:

We have set all that is on the earth as an adornment for it. (18:7)	*innā ja'alnā mā 'ala 'l-arḍi zīnatan la-hā.*

—and keep a safe distance from the perilous roads of the temptations of:

Your wealth and your children are merely a temptation. (64:15)	*innamā amwālu-kum wa awlādu-kum fitna.*

You must head for the routes that follow the courses of the guidance of:

This is surely a Reminder; so whoever is willing, let him choose a way to his Lord. (73:19)	*inna hādhihi tadhkira: fa-man shā'a 'ttakhadha ilā Rabbi-hi sabīlā.*

—and offer a supplication with the tongue of the urgent need of:

Is it not He who answers the distressed, when he calls unto Him? (27:62)	*am-man yujību 'l-muḍṭarra idhā da'ā-hu.*

—by saying, in humble entreaty and with a sense of personal incapacity:

Guide us in the straight path. (1:5)	*ihdina 'ṣ-ṣirāṭa 'l-mustaqīm.*

—until the herald of the ancient providential favor of:

As for the friends of Allāh, surely no fear shall be upon them, nor shall they grieve. (10:62)	*a-lā inna awliyā'a 'llāhi* *lā khawfun 'alai-him* *wa lā hum yaḥzanūn.*

—comes to meet you with the good tidings of the salutation of:

"Peace!"—such is the greeting from a Lord All-Compassionate. (36:58)	*salām: qawlan* *min Rabbin Raḥīm.*

—and carries you on the packhorse *[janība]* of:

Help from Allāh and a victory near at hand. (61:13)	*naṣrun mina 'llāhi* *wa fatḥun qarīb.*

—and invites you to enter the Gardens of the bliss of:

So they returned with grace and favor from Allāh (3:174)	*fa-'nqalabū bi-ni'matin* *mina 'llāhi wa faḍlin.*

Then the breeze of the fragrant aroma of loving union *[wiṣāl]* will blow from every side. The goblets of the drink of loving affection *[maḥabba]* will be passed around by the hands of the cupbearers of the Unseen *[suqāt al-ghaib]*, and the bearer of direct witness *[mushāhid ash-shuhūd]* will declare:

Behold, this is a reward for you. And your endeavor [upon earth] has found acceptance. (76:22)	*inna hādhā* *kāna la-kum jazā'an* *wa kāna sa'yu-kum* *mashkūrā.*

By night, the entertainer of intimate friendship *[munādim al-uns]* will weave the fascinating tale *[samar]* of:

And Allāh spoke directly to Moses. (4:164)	*wa kallama 'llāhu* *Mūsā taklīmā.*

He will paint such a vivid picture, in his elaboration of the scenario of:

Then, when his Lord revealed Himself to the mountain, [He caused it to crumble to dust]. (7:143)	*fa-lammā tajallā Rabbu-hu* *li'l-jabali* *[ja'ala-hu dakkan].*

—that his audience will experience, through the optic nerves of their perceptive faculties *[nawāẓir ʿuyūn al-baṣā'ir]*, the delirious raptures *[sakarāt]* of the spiritual states *[ḥālāt]* of:

> And Moses fell down swooning. (7:143) *wa kharra Mūsā ṣaʿiqā.*

Then, when they see for themselves the effects of the visions of:

> Faces on that day will be resplendent, *wujūhun yawmaʾidhin nāḍira :*
> looking toward their Lord. (75:22,23) *ilā Rabbi-hā nāẓira.*

—they will confess their personal inadequacy, and they will say, in the spiritual language that needs no ordinary words *[bi-lisān al-ḥāl]*:

> The eyes do not perceive Him, *lā tudriku-hu 'l-abṣāru*
> but He perceives the eyes. (6:103) *wa Huwa yudriku 'l-abṣār.*

The Tenth Letter

Concerning the need to shed tears, to acknowledge one's incapacity, to offer humble entreaty, and to seek refuge with Him (Exalted is He).

My dear friend!

If you do not place the forehead of urgent need upon the soil of admitted incapacity, and if the tears of sorrow do not rain down from the clouds of your eyes, the plants of your delight will not become verdant in the orchard of daily life. The gardens of men will not become fecundated to suit your purpose. The branches of patience *[ṣabr]* will not put forth the leaves of contentment *[riḍā]* and the fragrant perfumes of intimate friendship *[uns]*, nor will they bear the fruits of the nearness of:

And he enjoyed access to Our presence and a happy journey's end. (38:25)	*wa inna la-hu ʿinda-nā* *la-zulfā wa ḥusna maʾāb.*

You will fail to attain to the limit of perfection. The nightingales of your heart will not sing the melody of ardent longing, and the doves of your heart will not fly with the wings of:

I am going to my Lord: He will guide me. (37:99)	*innī dhāhibun ilā Rabbī* *sa-yahdī-n.*

—from the cage of:

Or shall man have whatever he may fancy? (53:24)	*am li'l-insāni* *mā tamannā.*

You will not cross the vast expanse of:

And do not strain your eyes toward that which We have given for some pairs among them to enjoy—the flower of this world's life, that We may thereby put them to the test. (20:131)	*wa lā tamuddanna ʿainai-ka* *ilā mā mattaʿnā bi-hi* *azwājan min-hum* *zahrata 'l-ḥayāti 'd-dunyā* *li-naftina-hum fī-h.*

You will fail to reach the lotus tree *[sidra]* of:

A sure abode, in the presence of a King All-Powerful. (54:55)	*maqʿadi ṣidqin* *ʿinda Malīkin Muqtadir.*

—and you will not gather any of the fruits of the trees of:

They shall have whatever they will in the presence of their Lord. (39:34) [19]	*la-hum mā yashāʾūna* *ʿinda Rabbi-him.*

No fragrant breeze will reach the nostrils of your heart from the orchard of:

And Allāh—with Him is the fairest journey's end. (3:14)	*wa 'llāhu ʿinda-hu* *ḥusnu 'l-maʾāb.*

—nor will your nose inhale the sweet scent of the roses of:

Theirs is the abode of peace with their Lord, and He will be their Protecting Friend because of what they used to do. (6:127)	*la-hum dāru 's-salāmi* *ʿinda Rabbi-him* *wa Huwa Waliyyu-hum* *bi-mā kānū yaʿmalūn.*

The Eleventh Letter

Concerning the affirmation of Oneness *[tawḥīd]* and the fruits thereof.

My dear friend!

When the glimmerings of the light of the dawn of the affirmation of Oneness *[tawḥīd]* first appear on our hearts, from the eastern horizons of:

By the dawn when it breathes a sigh. (81:18)	*wa 'ṣ-ṣubḥi* *idhā tanaffas.*

—and the suns of the eye of conviction *[ʿain al-yaqīn]* become established in the constellations of the spheres of:

And the sun runs on to a resting place of its own. (36:38)	*wa 'sh-shamsu tajrī* *li-mustaqarrin la-hā.*

—the darkness and gloom of human existence vanish, in the glow of the brilliant radiance of:

Their light will run in front of them. (66:8)	*nūru-hum yasʿā* *baina aidī-him.*

Revealed is the secret of:

He causes the night to pass into the day. (22:61)	*yūliju 'l-laila* *fi 'n-nahāri.*

—and the veil is lifted from the face of the foreordained gift of the grace of:

Allāh is the Protecting Friend of those who believe. He brings them out of the darkness into the light. (2:257)	*Allāhu Waliyyu 'lladhīna* *āmanū yukhriju-hum* *mina 'ẓ-ẓulumāti* *ila 'n-nūr.*

An attack is then mounted by the army of the devil of:

Surely Satan is an enemy to you . (35:6)	*inna 'sh-shaiṭāna la-kum ʿaduwwun.*

—on the battlefield of:

So treat him as an enemy. (35:6) — *fa-'ttakhidhū-hu ʿaduwwā.*

—with the assistance of the troops of:

Decked out fair for men is the love
of the pleasures derived
from women and children. (3:14)

zuyyina li'n-nāsi
ḥubbu 'sh-shahawāti
mina 'n-nisāʾi wa 'l-banīna.

—against the soldiers of the heart, who say:

Pardon us, forgive us, and have mercy
on us. You are our Protector,
so help us against
the disbelieving folk. (2:286)

wa ' ʿfu ʿan-nā
wa 'ghfir la-nā wa 'rḥam-nā:
Anta Mawlā-nā fa-'nṣur-nā
ʿala 'l-qawmi 'l-kāfirīn.

So the invisible herald of:

And with Him are the keys
of the Unseen. (6:59)

wa ʿinda-hu
mafātiḥu 'l-ghaibi.

—cries out:

Do not faint and do not grieve,
for you shall be the uppermost
[if you are true believers]. (3:139)

wa lā tahinū wa lā taḥzanū
wa antumu 'l-aʿlawna
[in kuntum muʾminīn].

They are soon reinforced by the troops of:

And Our host—they are sure
to be the victors. (37:173)

wa inna junda-nā
la-humu 'l-ghālibūn.

—with the announcement of:

When the help of Allāh comes,
and victory.... (110:1)[20]

idhā jāʾa naṣru 'llāhi
wa 'l-fatḥu....

—and advance notice of:

Surely We have given you
a clear victory. (48:1)

innā fataḥnā
la-ka fatḥan mubīnā.

They unsheathe the swords of:

Surely We shall help Our Messengers
and those who have believed. (40:51)

innā la-nanṣuru rusula-nā
wa 'lladhīna āmanū.

—from the scabbards of:

We raise by degrees
whomever We will. (12:76)

narfaʿu darajātin
man nashāʾ.

They launch an assault against the foes, and soon there are visible signs of:

So they routed them by Allāh's leave. (2:251)	*fa-hazamū-hum* *bi-idhni 'llāhi.*

Reports keep coming with the news of:

Help from Allāh and a victory near at hand. (61:13)	*naṣrun mina 'llāhi* *wa fatḥun qarīb.*

—and the herald of the spiritual state *[munādī 'l-ḥāl]* proclaims:

Say: "O Allāh! Owner of Sovereignty! You give sovereignty to whom You will, and You withdraw sovereignty from whom You will. You exalt whom You will, and You abase whom You will. In Your hand is all good. You are Able to do all things." (3:26)	*quli 'llāhumma Mālika 'l-Mulki* *tu'ti 'l-mulka man tashā'u* *wa tanzi'u 'l-mulka mim-man* *tashā': wa tu'izzu man tashā'u* *wa tudhillu man tashā':* *bi-yadi-ka 'l-khair:* *inna-ka 'alā kulli shai'in Qadīr.*

The Twelfth Letter

Concerning the urgent need for the companionship of the righteous *[ṣuḥbat al-abrār]*.

My dear friend!

You must extricate yourself from the dangerous predicament of:

Wealth and children are the adornment of the life of this world. (18:46)	*al-mālu wa 'l-banūna zīnatu 'l-ḥayāti 'd-dunyā.*

—and avoid the distraction of:

Our possessions and our families kept us preoccupied. (48:11)	*shagalat-nā amwālu-nā wa ahlū-nā.*

You must lift the foot of your aspiration out of the low-lying hollow of companionship with those who are cut off in the desert of the heedlessness of:

They have forgotten Allāh, so He has forgotten them. (9:67)	*nasu 'llāha fa-nasiya-hum.*

You must spur the racehorse of your quest in the arena of ardent love *[ʿishq]*, and swing the polo mallet of the plea for help of:

Appeal to Allāh for help. (7:128)	*istaʿīnū bi'llāhi.*

—to knock the ball of the prize of:

And the frontrunners, the frontrunners: those will be the ones brought near, [in the Gardens of Delight]. (56:10–12)	*wa 's-sābiqūna 's-sābiqūn: ulāʾika 'l-muqarrabūn: [fī jannāti 'n-naʿīm].*

—all the way to the goal of:

These follow guidance from their Lord, and it is they who will prosper. (2:5)	*ulāʾika ʿalā hudan min Rabbi-him wa ulāʾika humu 'l-mufliḥūn.*

Then maybe the imperial courier of:

And give those who believe the good tidings that they have a sure footing with their Lord. (10:2)	*wa bashshiri 'lladhīna āmanū* *anna la-hum qadama* *ṣidqin ʿinda Rabbi-him.*

—will cheer you with the good news that:

To human beings, Allāh is surely Ever-Gentle, All-Compassionate. (22:65)	*inna 'llāha bi 'n-nāsi* *la-Raʾūfun* *Raḥīm.*

—and give you the unsealed document of the secrets of:

Clear proofs have come to you from your Lord. (6:104)	*qad jāʾa-kum baṣāʾiru* *min Rabbi-kum.*

Then, once you have learned to decipher certain cryptic codes, you must move quickly, with the foot of your head, toward the roads of the safe passage *[subul salām]* of:

And this, the path of your Lord, is a straight path. (6:126)	*wa hādhā ṣirāṭu Rabbi-ka* *mustaqīmā.*

—and head for the recreation park *[muntazah]* of:

For them there are Gardens underneath which rivers flow. (2:25)	*[anna] la-hum jannātin tajrī* *min taḥti-ha 'l-anhār.*

You must ask for news of the eternal abode of the Gardens of Bliss, where:

They have degrees with their Lord, and forgiveness, and generous provision. (8:4)	*la-hum darajātun ʿinda Rabbi-him* *wa maghfiratun* *wa rizqun karīm.*

—for then the herald of the providential bounty of:

But as for those to whom the reward most fair has already gone forth from Us, [they shall be kept far from it (from Hell)]. (21:101)	*inna 'lladhīna sabaqat* *la-hum min-na 'l-ḥusnā:* *[ulāʾika ʿan-hā* *mubʿadūn].*

—will approach you and inform you, one by one, about all the domains of the Abode of Peace, where:

Allāh is well pleased with them, and they are well pleased with Him. (5:119)[21]	*raḍiya 'llāhu* *ʿan-hum* *wa raḍū ʿan-h.*

Then he will summon you to the throne of:

> And if someone fulfills his covenant made with Allāh, He will give him a mighty reward. (48:10)
>
> *wa man awfā bi-mā ʿāhada ʿalai-hu ʾllāha fa-sa-yuʾtī-hi ajran ʿaẓīmā.*

—and he will say:

> You will never attain to piety until you spend of that which you love. (3:92)
>
> *lan tanālū ʾl-birra ḥattā tunfiqū mim-mā tuḥibbūn.*

The Thirteenth Letter

Concerning the significance of the Qur'ānic verse [*āya*]:

Allāh is the Light of the heavens and the earth. (24:35)
[Allāhu nūru 's-samāwāti wa 'l-arḍ] [22]

—with reference to certain other verses [*āyāt*].

Dear brother!

When the brilliant rays of the lights of:

Allāh is the Light of the heavens and the earth. (24:35)	*Allāhu nūru 's-samāwāti wa 'l-arḍ.*

—start shining on the niche *[mishkāt]* of our consciences, the glass of the heart will be so affected by them that it sparkles with the light of:

The lamp is in a glass. The glass is as it were a shining star. (24:35)	*al-miṣbāḥu fī zujāja: az-zujājatu ka-anna-hā kawkabun durriyyun.*

The lightning flashes of the discoveries of:

[This lamp is] kindled from a blessed tree, [an olive]... (24:35)	*yūqadu min shajaratin mubārakatin [zaitūnatin]...*

—will gleam forth from the canopies of the clouds of:

neither of the East nor of the West... (24:35)	*lā sharqiyyatin wa lā gharbiyyatin...*

—and kindle the lamps of the concept of:

...whose oil whould almost glow forth [(of itself) though no fire touched it]. (24:35)	*yakādu zaitu-hā yuḍī'u [wa law lam tamsas-hu nār].*

The skies of our innermost beings will then be adorned, in their entirety, with the stars of the wisdom of:

And by the stars they are guided. (16:16)	*wa bi'n-najmi hum yahtadūn.*

—and with the planets of the embellishment of:

We have adorned the lowest heaven with the adornment of the planets. (37:6)	*innā* *zayyanna 's-samā'a 'd-dunya* *bi-zīnatini 'l-kawākib.*

The moons of present awareness *[ḥuḍūr]* will rise from the horizons of:

Light upon light. (24:35)	*nūrun 'alā nūr.*

—and ascend to the constellations of the lofty elevation of:

And for the moon We have appointed mansions. (36:39)	*wa 'l-qamara qaddarnā-hu* *manāzila.*

—so that the nights of the heedlessness of:

By the night when it is enshrouding. (92:1)	*wa 'l-laili* *idhā yaghshā.*

—acquire the quality of:

And the day when it is resplendent. (92:2)	*wa 'n-nahāri* *idhā tajallā.*

The fragrant perfumes of remembrance *[dhikr]* will emanate from the blessed grace of:

Those who seek forgiveness in the watches of the night. (3:17)	*al-mustaghfirīna* *bi'l-asḥār.*

The nightingales *[balābil]* of the trees of:

They used to sleep only a little during the night. (51:17)	*kānū qalīlan mina 'l-laili* *mā yahja'ūn.*

—will sing their melodious songs of sorrow and grief, until the dawn of the good fortune of:

Allāh guides to His light whomever He will. (24:35)	*yahdi 'llāhu* *li-nūri-hi man yashā'.*

—makes its appearance, and the suns of the insights of direct knowledge *[shumūs al-ma'ārif]* begin their ascension from the point of:

He whom Allāh guides, he is indeed the one who is guided aright. (7:178)	*man yahdi 'llāhu* *fa-huwa 'l-muhtadī.*

Into plain view will then emerge the mysteries of:

It is not for the sun to overtake the moon, nor does the night outstrip the day.	*la 'sh-shamsu* *yanbaghī la-hā* *an yudrika 'l-qamara wa la 'l-lailu*

They are floating each in a separate orbit. (36:40)	*sābiqu 'n-nahār:* *wa kullun fī falakin yasbaḥūn.*

—and disclosed from the shapes of concealment will be the subtle enigmas of the secrets of:

And Allāh speaks to mankind in allegories, for Allāh is Knower of all things. (24:35)	*wa yaḍribu 'llāhu 'l-amthāla* *li'n-nās:* *wa 'llāhu bi-kulli shai'in ʿAlīm.*

The Fourteenth Letter

Concerning the perfection of direct knowledge *[maʿrifa]*, the perfection of religion *[dīn]*, and the fruits of thereof.

My dear friend!

When the sun of the sky of direct knowledge *[maʿrifa]* has reached the constellations of the perfection of:

Today I have perfected your religion for you. (5:3)	*al-yawma akmaltu la-kum dīna-kum.*

—and the sun of loving affection *[yūḥ al-maḥabba]* has ascended to the point of complete surveillance over the highway systems of:

And I have completed My blessing upon you. (5:3)	*wa atmamtu ʿalai-kum niʿmatī.*

—the brilliant rays of the lights of:

And I have approved Islām for you as religion. (5:3)	*wa raḍītu la-kumu 'l-islāma dīnā.*

—will shine forth, and the eye of certainty *[ʿain al-yaqīn]* will witness the explicit proofs of the implications of:

Is he whose breast Allāh has expanded to receive Islām, so that he is guided by a light from his Lord...? (39:22)	*a-fa-man sharaḥa 'llāhu ṣadra-hu li'l-islāmi fa-huwa ʿalā nūrin min Rabbi-h.*

—in the sublime demonstration of:

The truth has come to you from your Lord. (10:94)	*la-qad jāʾa-ka 'l-ḥaqqu min Rabbi-ka.*

It will discover the hidden treasures of the secrets of:

And unto Allāh belong the treasuries of the heavens and of the earth. (63:7)	*wa li'llāhi khazāʾinu 's-samāwāti wa 'l-arḍi.*

—and survey the subtle details of the real meanings *[daqā'iq ḥaqā'iq]* of:

And in the earth there are signs for those who have sure faith, as well as in your own selves. What, do you not see? (51:20,21)	*wa fi 'l-arḍi āyātun li'l-mūqinīn: wa fī anfusi-kum a-fa-lā tubṣirūn.*

—and become privy to the enigmatic indications of:

So whichever way you turn, there is the Face of Allāh. (2:115)	*fa-aina-mā tuwallū fa-thamma wajhu 'llāh.*

The winds of the copious bounty of:

And We send the winds fertilizing. (15:22)	*wa arsalna 'r-riyāḥa lawāqiḥa.*

—will blow, and so will the winds of the gracious favor of:

We visit with Our mercy whom We will, and We leave not to waste the reward of those who do good. (12:56)	*nuṣību bi-raḥmati-nā man nashā'u wa lā nuḍī'u ajra 'l-muḥsinīn.*

—from the direction of:

Allāh is Ever-Gentle to His servants. (42:19)	*Allāhu Laṭīfun bi-'ibādi-hi.*

—in the orchards of:

We do not leave to waste the reward of one who does good works. (18:30)	*innā lā nuḍī'u ajra man aḥsana 'amalā.*

The trees of the gardens of:

Surely Allāh is with those who are careful of their duty to Him, and those who are doers of good. (16:128)	*inna 'llāha ma'a 'lladhīna 'ttaqaw wa 'lladhīna hum muḥsinūn.*

—will put forth the leaves of direct perception *[shuhūd]*, and they will bear the fruits of manifestation *[tajallī]* to the utmost limit of perfection.

The fountains of the attainment of:

Such is the bounty of Allāh; He bestows it on whom He will. (62:4)	*dhālika faḍlu 'llāhi yu'tī-hi man yashā'.*

—will flow from the heights of the mountains of:

Allāh is the Lord of infinite bounty. (62:4)	*wa 'llāhu Dhu 'l-faḍli 'l-'aẓīm.*

—into the river bed of the valleys of the heart.

Then the mysterious voice of the Unseen *[hātif al-ghaib]* will use the tongues of creatures to let it be known that:

As for those who believe and do righteous deeds, the All-Merciful will surely assign them love. (19:96)	*inna 'lladhīna āmanū* *wa ʿamilu 'ṣ-ṣāliḥāti sa-yajʿalu* *la-humu 'r-Raḥmānu wuddā.*

The herald of good fortune will pronounce the good tidings of:

O My servants, for you there is no fear this Day, and you are not the ones who will be feeling sad. (43:68)	*yā ʿibādi lā khawfun* *ʿalai-kumu 'l-yawma* *wa lā antum taḥzanūn.*

—and Riḍwān [the custodian of the Garden of Paradise] will come to meet them from the abodes of:

A fair land, and an All-Forgiving Lord. (34:15)	*baldatun ṭayyibatun* *wa Rabbun Ghafūr.*

—and he will say:

And therein you shall have all that you yourselves desire, and therein you shall have all that you call for, as an offering of hospitality from One who is All-Forgiving, All-Compassionate. (41:31,32)	*wa la-kum fī-hā* *mā tashtahī anfusu-kum* *wa la-kum fī-hā* *mā taddaʿūn:* *nuzulan min* *Ghafūrin Raḥīm.*

The Fifteenth Letter

Concerning the benefits of a sound heart *[qalb salīm]*, a whole mind *[ʿaql kāmil]* and a genuine conviction *[yaqīn ṣādiq]*.

My dear friend!

It is vital for the seeker to have a sound heart, in order to grasp the implications of:

So pay attention, O you who have eyes! (59:2)	*fa-'ʿtabirū* *yā uli 'l-abṣār.*

—and a whole mind, in order to comprehend the subtle secrets of:

We shall show them Our signs on the horizons and within themselves. (41:53)	*sa-nurī-him āyāti-nā fi 'l-āfāqi* *wa fī anfusi-him.*

—and a genuine conviction, in order to inspect with the eye of the heart all aspects of the realization that:

There is not a thing that does not celebrate His praise, and yet you do not understand their celebration. (17:44)	*wa in min shaiʾin* *illā yusabbiḥu bi-ḥamdi-hi* *wa lākin lā tafqahūna* *tasbīḥa-hum.*

He must receive with his heart the means of connecting with:

And when My servants question you concerning Me, I am Near. I answer the call of the caller, when he calls to Me. (2:186)	*wa idhā saʾala-ka* *ʿibādī ʿannī fa-innī Qarīb:* *ujību daʿwata 'd-dāʿī* *idhā daʿā-ni.*

He must wake up from the heedlessness of:

And let hope beguile them, for they will soon come to know! (15:3)	*wa yulhi-himu 'l-amalu* *fa-sawfa yaʿlamūn.*

He must escape the chidings of the admonition:

What, did you suppose that We had created you for idle sport, and that you would not be returned to Us? (23:115)	*a-fa-ḥasibtum anna-mā* *khalaqnā-kum ʿabathan* *wa anna-kum* *ilai-nā lā turjaʿūn.*

—by grasping the most secure handle *[ʿurwa wuthqā]*[23] of:

And, apart from Allāh, you have no protecting friend or helper. (9:116)[24]	*wa mā la-kum min dūni 'llāhi min waliyyin wa lā naṣīr.*

—and boarding the ship of:

So flee unto Allāh. (51:50)	*fa-firrū ila 'llāh.*

—on the ocean of the wave of:

I have not created the jinn and humankind except to serve Me. (51:56)	*wa mā khalaqtu 'l-jinna wa 'l-insa illā li-yaʿbudūn.*

He must plunge deep into the ocean, risking his breath of life, for then, if he gains the jewel sought:

He has truly won a mighty triumph. (33:71)	*fa-qad fāza fawzan ʿaẓīmā.*

—and if his lifeblood *[muhja]* is destroyed:

His reward will then be incumbent upon Allāh. (4:100)	*fa-qad waqaʿa ajru-hu ʿala 'llāh.*

Praise be to Allāh, and to Him alone, and may Allāh bless the one after whom there will be no other Prophet.

The conclusion of the transcription of these letters occurred in the daytime of Thursday, the 4th of the sacred month of Dhu'l-Qaʿda, in the year [A.H.] 1077, at the hand of the servant who stands in dire need of the One who is fully Aware of his faults:

Ismāʿīl ibn Ayyūb ibn Aḥmad ibn Ayyūb,
member of the Khalwatī Order *[Ṭarīqa]*
and follower of the Ḥanafī [school of Islamic law].

May Allāh treat him with His mysterious kindness.
Āmīn, O Lord of All the Worlds!

Notes

[1] This is an allusion to the Qur'ānic story of Noah (peace be upon him) and his ark, where Allāh (Exalted is He has told us):

And it was said: "O earth, swallow	*wa qīla yā arḍu 'blaʿī*
your water, and O sky , abate	*māʾa-ki wa yā samāʾu aqliʿī*
your downpour!" And the water	*wa ghīḍa 'l-māʾu*
was made to subside. The affair was	*wa quḍiya 'l-amru*
accomplished, and it [the ark] came	*wa 'stawat*
to rest upon [Mount] al-Jūdī. (11:44)	*ʿala 'l-Jūdiyyi.*

According to the traditional Qur'ānic commentators, al-Jūdī is the name of a mountain in the Jazīra region of Mesopotamia, near the town of Mosul on the Tigris.

[2] The expression *maqʿad ṣidq* [lit., seat of truthfulness] occurs in the Qur'ānic verses:

The righteous will surely dwell	*inna 'l-muttaqīna fī jannātin*
amid gardens and a river,	*wa nahar:*
in a sure abode, in the presence	*fī maqʿadi ṣidqin*
of a King All-Powerful. (54:54,55)	*ʿinda Malīkin Muqtadir.*

[3] This is not a Qur'ānic verse.

[4] An almost identical expression occurs in Q. 26:213

[5] These words of Allāh (Exalted is He) occur also in Q. 5:119, 9:100, and 58:22.

[6] These words of Allāh (Exalted is He) occur also in Q. 48:7.

[7] In full, this Qur'ānic verse *[āya]* reads as follows:

You cause the night to pass	*tūliju 'l-laila*
into the day, and You cause	*fī 'n-nahāri*
the day to pass into the night.	*wa tūliju 'n-nahāra fī 'l-lail:*
You bring forth the living from	*wa tukhriju 'l-ḥayya*
the dead, and You bring forth	*mina 'l-mayyiti*
the dead from the living.	*wa tukhriju 'l-mayyita*
And you give sustenance	*mina 'l-ḥayyi*
to whom You choose,	*wa tarzuqu man tashāʾu*
without reckoning. (3:27)	*bi-ghairi ḥisāb.*

[8] An allusion to the words of Allāh (Exalted is He):

Iram of the many columns,	*Irama dhāti 'l-'imād:*
the like of which was never	*allatī lam yukhlaq*
created in the lands. (89:7,8)	*mithlu-hā fi 'l-bilād.*

[9] These words of Allāh (Exalted is He) are also to be found in 24:54, 47:33 and 64:12.

[10] In full, this verse *[āya]* of the Qur'ān reads as follows:

On the day when the earth	*yawma*
will be changed to other than	*tubaddalu 'l-arḍu*
this earth, and the heavens	*ghaira 'l-arḍi*
[will also be changed], and they	*wa 's-samāwātu*
will come forth unto Allāh, the One,	*wa barazū*
the All-Compelling.* (14:48)	*li'llāhi 'l-Wāḥidi 'l-Qahhār.**

* Note the use of the abstract noun *qahhāriyya* [all-compelling nature] in the heading to the Sixth Letter (p. 20 above).

[11] While the expression *haba'an manthūrā* occurs in the Qur'ānic verse *[āya]*:

And We shall advance upon the work	*wa qadimnā ilā mā 'amilū*
they have done, and make it into	*min 'amalin fa-ja'alnā-hu*
scattered particles of dust. (25:23)	*habā'an manthūrā.*

—the more obvious allusion here is to the virtually synonymous expression *haba'an munbaththa*, as it occurs in the context of the words of Allāh (Exalted is He):

And the mountains will be ground	*wa bussati 'l-jibālu*
to powder, so that they become	*bassā: fa-kānat*
a scattered dust. (56:5,6)	*haba'an munbaththā.*

[12] Isrāfīl (peace be upon him) is the angel who is charged with the task of sounding the trumpet on the Day of Resurrection.

[13] The pronoun "them" refers to those of whom Allāh (Exalted is He) has said:

As for those to whom the reward	*inna 'lladhīna*
most fair has already gone forth	*sabaqat la-hum*
from Us, they will be far	*min-na 'l-ḥusnā*
removed from it [from Hell]. (21:101)	*ulā'ika 'an-hā mub'adūn.*

[14] In the words of Allāh (Almighty and Glorious is He):

The register of the righteous	*kallā inna kitāba 'l-abrāri*
is in *'Illiyyūn*. Ah, what will	*la-fī 'Illiyyīn:*
convey to you what *'Illiyyūn* is?	*wa mā adrā-ka*
A written record, attested to	*mā 'Illiyyūn:*
by those who are brought	*kitābun marqūm:*
near [unto their Lord] (83:18-21)	*yashhadu-hu 'l-muqarrabūn.*

According to a tradition *[ḥadīth]* recorded in *Mishkāt al-Masābīḥ*, the Prophet (Allāh bless him and give him peace) once said:

> The angels follow the soul through each of the heavens, and the angels of one region pass it on to the next, until it reaches the seventh heaven, when Allāh (Exalted is He) says: "Record the name of My servant in *ʿIlliyyūn*, then return him to the earth, that is, to his body which is buried in the earth."

15 See note 2 on p. 48 above.

16 In full, this verse *[āya]* of the Qurʾān reads as follows:

Good news for you this day:	*bushrā-kumu 'l-yawma jannātun*
Gardens underneath which rivers flow,	*tajrī min taḥti-ha 'l-anhāru*
wherein you shall dwell forever.	*khālidīna fī-hā:*
That is the supreme triumph. (57:12)	*dhālika huwa 'l-fawzu 'l-ʿaẓīm.*

17 These words of Allāh (Exalted is He) occur also in Q. 8:10.

18 These words of Allāh (Exalted is He) occur also in Q. 68:44.

19 These words of Allāh (Exalted is He) occur also in Q. 42:22.

20 This is the first verse *[āya]* of the short Sūra entitled *an-Naṣr* [Help], which reads in full:

When the help of Allāh comes,	*idhā jāʾa naṣru 'llāhi*
and victory, and you see mankind	*wa 'l-fatḥu*
entering the religion of Allāh	*wa raʾaita 'n-nāsa yadkhulūna*
in throngs, then proclaim the praise	*fī dīni 'llāhi afwājā: fa-sabbiḥ*
of your Lord, and seek His forgiveness;	*bi-ḥamdi Rabbi-ka wa 'staghfir-h:*
for He is Ever-Relenting. (110:1–3)	*inna-hu kāna Tawwābā.*

21 These words of Allāh (Exalted is He) occur also in Q. 9:100, 58:22 and 98:8.

22 In its entirety, this Qurʾānic verse *[āya]* reads as follows:

Allāh is the Light of the heavens and	*Allāhu nūru 's-samāwāti wa 'l-arḍ:*
the earth. The similitude of His light	*mathalu nūri-hi*
is as a niche wherein is a lamp.	*ka-mishkātin fī-hā miṣbāḥ:*
The lamp is in a glass.	*al-miṣbāḥu fī zujāja:*
The glass is as it were a shining star.	*az-zujājatu ka-anna-hā kawkabun*
[This lamp is] kindled	*durriyyun yūqadu min shajaratin*
from a blessed tree, an olive	*mubārakatin zaitūnatin*
neither of the East nor of the West,	*lā sharqiyyatin wa lā gharbiyyatin*
whose oil whould almost glow forth	*yakādu zaitu-hā yuḍīʾu*
[of itself] though no fire touched it.	*wa law lam tamsas-hu nār:*
Light upon light. Allāh guides	*nūrun ʿalā nūr: yahdi 'llāhu*
to His light whom He will. And Allāh	*li-nūri-hi man yashāʾ:*
speaks to mankind in allegories, for	*wa yaḍribu 'llāhu 'l-amthāla li'n-nās:*
Allāh is Knower of all things. (24:35)	*wa 'llāhu bi-kulli shaiʾin ʿAlīm.*

[23] This is an allusion to the verse *[āya]* of the Qur'ān:

There is no compulsion in religion.	*lā ikrāha fi 'd-dīn:*
The right direction is henceforth	*qad tabayyana 'r-rushdu*
distinct from error.	*mina 'l-ghayy:*
And he who rejects false deities	*fa-man yakfur bi'ṭ-ṭāghūti*
and believes in Allāh has grasped	*wa yu'min bi'llāhi fa-qadi 'stamsaka*
the most secure handle,	*bi'l-'urwati 'l-wuthqā*
which will never break. (2:256)	*la 'nfiṣāma la-hā.*

[24] These words of Allāh (Exalted is He) occur also in Q. 29:22 and 42:31.

Concerning the Author, Shaikh ʿAbd al-Qādir al-Jīlānī

A Brief Introduction by the Translator[1]

The Author's Names and Titles

A rich store of information about the author of *Fifteen Letters* is conveniently available, to those familiar with the religious and spiritual tradition of Islām, in his names, his surnames, and the many titles conferred upon him by his devoted followers. It is not unusual for these to take up several lines in an Arabic manuscript, but let us start with the short form of the author's name as it appears on the cover and title page of this book: *Shaikh ʿAbd al-Qādir al-Jīlānī*.

Shaikh: A term applied throughout the Islamic world to respected persons of recognized seniority in learning, experience and wisdom. Its basic meaning in Arabic is "an elder; a man over fifty years of age." (The spellings *Sheikh* and *Shaykh* may also be encountered in English-language publications.)

ʿ*Abd al-Qādir:* This is the author's personal name, meaning "Servant [or Slave] of the All-Powerful." (The form *ʿAbdul Qādir*, which the reader may come across elsewhere, is simply an alternative transliteration of the Arabic spelling.) It has always been a common practice, in the Muslim community, to give a male child a name in which *ʿAbd* is prefixed to one of the Names of Allāh.

[1] Reproduced for the convenience of the reader, with slight modifications from the version printed on pp. xiii-xix of: Shaikh ʿAbd al-Qādir. *Revelations of the Unseen (Futūḥ al-Ghaib)*. Translated from the Arabic by Muhtar Holland. Houston, Texas: Al-Baz Publishing, Inc., 1992.

al-Jīlānī: A surname ending in *-ī* will often indicate the bearer's place of birth. Shaikh ʿAbd al-Qādir was born in the Iranian district of Gīlān, south of the Caspian Sea, in A.H. 470/1077-8 C.E. (In some texts, the Persian spelling *Gīlānī* is used instead of the arabicized form al-Jīlānī. The abbreviated form *al-Jīlī*, which may also be encountered, should not be confused with the surname of the venerable ʿAbd al-Karīm al-Jīlī, author of the celebrated work al-Insān al-Kāmil, who came from Jīl in the district of Baghdād.)

Let us now consider a slightly longer version of the Shaikh's name, as it occurs near the beginning of *Al-Fatḥ ar-Rabbānī [The Sublime Revelation]: Sayyidunā 'sh-Shaikh Muḥyi'd-Dīn Abū Muḥammad ʿAbd al-Qādir (Raḍiya'llāhu ʿanh)*.

Sayyidunā 'sh-Shaikh: "Our Master, the Shaikh." A writer who regards himself as a Qādirī, a devoted follower of Shaikh ʿAbd al-Qādir, will generally refer to the latter as *Sayyidunā* [our Master], or *Sayyidī* [my Master].

Muḥyi'd-Dīn: "Reviver of the Religion." It is widely acknowledged by historians, non-Muslim as well as Muslim, that Shaikh ʿAbd al-Qādir displayed great courage in reaffirming the traditional teachings of Islām, in an era when sectarianism was rife, and when materialistic and rationalistic tendencies were predominant in all sections of society. In matters of Islamic jurisprudence *[fiqh]* and theology *[kalām]*, he adhered quite strictly to the highly "orthodox" school of Imām Aḥmad ibn Ḥanbal.

Abū Muḥammad: "Father of Muḥammad." In the Arabic system of nomenclature, a man's surnames usually include the name of his first-born son, with the prefix *Abū* [Father of—].

Raḍiya'llāhu ʿanh: "May Allāh be well pleased with him!" This benediction is the one customarily pronounced—and spelled out in writing—after mentioning the name of a Companion of the Prophet (Allāh bless him and give him peace). The preference for this particular invocation is yet another mark of the extraordinary status held by Shaikh ʿAbd al-Qādir in the eyes of his devoted followers.

Finally, we must note some important elements contained within this even longer version: *al-Ghawth al-Aʿẓam Sulṭān al-Awliyāʾ Sayyidunā 'sh-Shaikh Muḥyi'd-Dīn ʿAbd al-Qādir al-Jīlānī al-Ḥasanī al-Ḥusainī (Raḍiya'llāhu ʿanh)*.

al-Ghawth al-Aʿẓam: "The Supreme Helper" (or, "The Mightiest Succor"). *Ghawth* is an Arabic word meaning: (1) A cry for aid or succor. (2) Aid, help, succor; deliverance from adversity. (3) The chief of the Saints, who is empowered by Allāh to bring succor to suffering humanity, in response to His creatures' cry for help in times of extreme adversity.

Sulṭān al-Awliyāʾ: "The Sultan of the Saints." This reinforces the preceding title, emphasizing the supremacy of the *Ghawth* above all other orders of sanctity.

al-Ḥasanī al-Ḥusainī: "The descendant of both al-Ḥasan and al-Ḥusain, the grandsons of the Prophet (Allāh bless him and give him peace)." To quote the Turkish author, Shaikh Muzaffer Ozak Efendi (may Allāh bestow His mercy upon him): "The lineage of Shaikh ʿAbd al-Qādir is known as the Chain of Gold, since both his parents were descendants of the Messenger (Allāh bless him and give him peace). His noble father, ʿAbdullāh, traced his descent by way of Imām Ḥasan, while his revered mother, Umm al-Khair, traced hers through Imām Ḥusain."

As for the many other surnames, titles and honorific appellations that have been conferred upon Shaikh ʿAbd al-Qādir al-Jīlānī, it may suffice at this point to mention *al-Bāz al-Ashhab* [The Gray Falcon].

The Author's Life in Baghdād

Through the mists of legend surrounding the life of Shaikh ʿAbd al-Qādir al-Jīlānī, it is possible to discern the outlines of the following biographical sketch:

In A.H. 488, at the age of eighteen, he left his native province to become a student in the great capital city of Baghdād, the hub of political, commercial and cultural activity, and the center of religious learning in the world of Islām. After studying traditional sciences under such teachers as the prominent Ḥanbalī jurist *[faqīh]*, Abū Sa'd 'Alī al-Mukharrimī, he encountered a more spiritually oriented instructor in the saintly person of Abu'l-Khair Ḥammād ad-Dabbās. Then, instead of embarking on his own professorial career, he abandoned the city and spent twenty-five years as a wanderer in the desert regions of 'Irāq.

He was over fifty years old by the time he returned to Baghdād, in A.H. 521/1127 C.E., and began to preach in public. His hearers were profoundly affected by the style and content of his lectures, and his reputation grew and spread through all sections of society. He moved into the school *[madrasa]* belonging to his old teacher al-Mukharrimī, but the premises eventually proved inadequate. In A.H. 528, pious donations were applied to the construction of a residence and guesthouse *[ribāṭ]*, capable of housing the Shaikh and his large family, as well as providing accommodation for his pupils and space for those who came from far and wide to attend his regular sessions *[majālis]*.

He lived to a ripe old age, and continued his work until his very last breath, as we know from the accounts of his final moments recorded in the Addendum to Revelations of the Unseen.

In the words of Shaikh Muzaffer Ozak Efendi: "The venerable 'Abd al-Qādir al-Jīlānī passed on to the Realm of Divine Beauty in A.H. 561/1166 C.E., and his blessed mausoleum in Baghdād is still a place of pious visitation. He is noted for his extraordinary spiritual experiences and exploits, as well as his memorable sayings and wise teachings. It is rightly said of him that 'he was born in love, grew in perfection, and met his Lord in the perfection of love.' May the All-Glorious Lord bring us in contact with his lofty spiritual influence!"

The Author's Literary Works

***Al-Fatḥ ar-Rabbānī* [The Sublime Revelation].** A collection of sixty-two discourses delivered by Shaikh 'Abd al-Qādir in the years A.H. 545-546/1150-1152 C.E. Arabic text published by Dār al-Albāb, Damascus, n.d. Arabic text with Urdu translation: Madīna Publishing Co.,

Karachi, 1989. Translated from the Arabic by Muhtar Holland. Houston, Texas: Al-Baz Publishing, Inc., 1992.

Even a non-Muslim scholar like D.S. Margoliouth was so favorably impressed by the content and style of *Al-Fatḥ ar-Rabbānī* that he wrote:[2] "The sermons included in [this work] are some of the very best in Muslim literature: the spirit which they breathe is one of charity and philanthropy: the preacher would like to 'close the gates of Hell and open those of Paradise to all mankind.' He employs Ṣūfī technicalities very rarely, and none that would occasion the ordinary reader much difficulty...."

***Malfūẓāt* [Utterances].** A loosely organized compilation of talks and sayings by Shaikh ʿAbd al-Qādir, almost equal in total length to Revelations of the Unseen. Frequently treated as a kind of appendix or supplement to manuscript and printed versions of *Al-Fatḥ ar-Rabbānī*. Translated from the Arabic by Muhtar Holland. Houston, Texas: Al-Baz Publishing, Inc., 1992.

***Futūḥ al-Ghaib* [Revelations of the Unseen].** A collection of seventy-eight discourses. The Arabic text, edited by Muḥammad Sālim al-Bawwāb, has been published by Dār al-Albāb, Damascus, 1986. German translation: W. Braune. *Die Futūḥ al-Gaib des ʿAbd al-Qādir*. Berlin and Leipzig: Walter de Gruyter & Co., 1933. English translations: (1) M. Aftab-ud-Din Ahmad. *Futuh Al-Ghaib [The Revelations of the Unseen]*. Lahore, Pakistan: Sh. Muhammad Ashraf. Repr. 1986. (2) Shaikh ʿAbd al-Qādir al-Jīlānī. *Revelations of the Unseen (Futūḥ al-Ghaib)*. Translated from the Arabic by Muhtar Holland. Houston, Texas: Al-Baz Publishing, Inc., 1992.

***Sirr al-Asrār* [The Secret of Secrets].** A short work, divided into twenty-four chapters, in which "the realities within our faith and our path are divulged." English translation: *The Secret of Secrets by Ḥaḍrat ʿAbd al-Qādir al-Jīlānī*, interpreted by Shaykh Tosun Bayrak al-Jerrahi al-Halveti. Cambridge, England: The Islamic Texts Society, 1992.

[2] In his article "ʿAbd al-Ḳādir" in Encyclopaedia of Islam (also printed in Shorter Encyclopaedia of Islam. Leiden, Netherlands: E.J. Brill, 1961).

Jalāʾ al-Khawāṭir **[The Removal of Cares]**. A collection of forty-five discourses by Shaikh ʿAbd al-Qādir. Arabic text with Urdu translation published by Maktaba Nabawiyya, Lahore, n.d. Translated from the Arabic by Muhtar Holland. Ft. Lauderdale, Florida: Al-Baz Publishing, Inc., 1997.

Al-Ghunya li-Ṭālibī Ṭarīq al-Ḥaqq **[Sufficient Provision for Seekers of the Path of Truth].** Arabic text published in two parts by Dār al-Albāb, Damascus, n.d., 192 pp. + 200 pp. Translated from the Arabic (in 5 vols.) by Muhtar Holland. Ft. Lauderdale, Florida: Al-Baz Publishing, Inc., 1997.

Khamsata ʿAshara Maktūban **[Fifteen Letters].** Translated from Persian into Arabic by ʿAlī ibn Ḥusāmu 'd-dīn al-Muttaqī, and from Arabic into English by Muhtar Holland. Hollywood, Florida: Al-Baz Publishing, Inc., 1997

Other works attributed to Shaikh ʿAbd al-Qādir include short treatises on some of the Divine Names; litanies *[awrād/aḥzāb]*; prayers and supplications *[daʿawāt/munājāt]*; mystical poems *[qaṣāʾid]*.

May Allāh forgive our mistakes and failings, and may He bestow His blessings upon all connected with our project—especially our gracious readers! Āmīn.

Muhtar Holland

About the Translator

Muhtar Holland was born in 1935, in the ancient city of Durham in the North East of England. This statement may be considered anachronistic, however, since he did not bear the name Muhtar until 1969, when he was moved—by powerful experiences in the *latihan kejiwaan* of Subud—to embrace the religion of Islām.*

At the age of four, according to an entry in his father's diary, he said to a man who asked his name: "I'm a stranger to myself." During his years at school, he was drawn most strongly to the study of languages, which seemed to offer signposts to guide the stranger on his "Journey Home," apart from their practical usefulness to one who loved to spend his vacations traveling—at first on a bicycle—through foreign lands. Serious courses in Latin, Greek, French, Spanish and Danish, with additional smatterings of Anglo-Saxon, Italian, German and Dutch. Travels in France, Germany, Belgium, Holland and Denmark. Then a State Scholarship and up to Balliol College, Oxford, for a degree course centered on the study of Arabic and Turkish. Travels in Turkey and Syria. Then National Service in the Royal Navy, with most of the two years spent on an intensive course in the Russian language.

In the years since graduation from Oxford and Her Majesty's Senior Service, Mr. Holland has held academic posts at the University of Toronto, Canada; at the School of Oriental and African Studies in the University of London, England (with a five-month leave to study Islamic Law in Cairo, Egypt); and at the Universiti Kebangsaan in Kuala Lumpur, Malaysia (followed by a six-month sojourn in Indonesia). He also worked as Senior Research Fellow at the Islamic Foundation in Leicester, England, and as Director of the Nūr al-Islām Translation Center in Valley Cottage, New York.

* The name Muhtar was received at that time from Bapak Muhammad Subuh Sumohadiwidjojo, of Wisma Subud, Jakarta, in response to a request for a suitable Muslim name. In strict academic transliteration from the Arabic, the spelling would be *Mukhtār*. The form *Muchtar* is probably more common in Indonesia than *Muhtar*, which happens to coincide with the modern Turkish spelling of the name.

His freelance activities have mostly been devoted to writing and translating in various parts of the world, including Scotland and California. He made his Pilgrimage *[Ḥajj]* to Mecca in 1980.

Published works include the following:

Al-Ghazālī. *On the Duties of Brotherhood*. Translated from the Classical Arabic by Muhtar Holland. London: Latimer New Dimensions, 1975. New York: Overlook Press, 1977. Repr. 1980 and 1993.

Sheikh Muzaffer Ozak al-Jerrahi. *The Unveiling of Love*. Translated from the Turkish by Muhtar Holland. New York: Inner Traditions, 1981. Westport, Ct.: Pir Publications, 1990.

Ibn Taymīya. *Public Duties in Islām*. Translated from the Arabic by Muhtar Holland. Leicester, England: Islamic Foundation, 1982.

Hasan Shushud. *Masters of Wisdom of Central Asia*. Translated from the Turkish by Muhtar Holland. Ellingstring, England: Coombe Springs Press, 1983.

Al-Ghazālī. *Inner Dimensions of Islamic Worship*. Translated from the Arabic by Muhtar Holland. Leicester, England: Islamic Foundation, 1983.

Sheikh Muzaffer Ozak al-Jerrahi. *Irshād*. Translated [from the Turkish] with an Introduction by Muhtar Holland. Warwick, New York: Amity House, 1988. Westport, Ct.: Pir Publications, 1990.

Sheikh Muzaffer Ozak al-Jerrahi. *Blessed Virgin Mary*. Translation from the Original Turkish by Muhtar Holland. Westport, Ct.: Pir Publications, 1991.

Sheikh Muzaffer Ozak al-Jerrahi. *The Garden of Dervishes*. Translation from the Original Turkish by Muhtar Holland. Westport, Ct.: Pir Publications, 1991.

Sheikh Muzaffer Ozak al-Jerrahi. *Adornment of Hearts*. Translation from the Original Turkish by Muhtar Holland and Sixtina Friedrich. Westport, Ct.: Pir Publications, 1991.

Sheikh Muzaffer Ozak al-Jerrahi. *Ashki's Divan*. Translation from the Original Turkish by Muhtar Holland and Sixtina Friedrich. Westport, Ct.: Pir Publications, 1991.

Shaikh ʿAbd al-Qādir al-Jīlānī. *Revelations of the Unseen (Futūḥ al-Ghaib)*. Translated from the Arabic by Muhtar Holland. Houston, Texas: Al-Baz Publishing, Inc., 1992

Shaikh ʿAbd al-Qādir al-Jīlānī. *The Sublime Revelation (al-Fatḥ ar-Rabbānī)*. Translated from the Arabic by Muhtar Holland. Houston, Texas: Al-Baz Publishing, Inc., 1992

Shaikh ʿAbd al-Qādir al-Jīlānī. *Utterances (Malfūẓāt)*. Translated from the Arabic by Muhtar Holland. Houston, Texas: Al-Baz Publishing, Inc., 1992

Shaikh ʿAbd al-Qādir al-Jīlānī. *The Removal of Cares (Jalāʾ al-Khawāṭir)*. Translated from the Arabic by Muhtar Holland. Ft. Lauderdale, Florida: Al-Baz Publishing, Inc., 1997

Shaikh ʿAbd al-Qādir al-Jīlānī. *Sufficient Provision for Seekers of the Path of Truth (Al-Ghunya li-Ṭālibī Ṭariq al-Ḥaqq)*. Translated from the Arabic (in 5 vols.) by Muhtar Holland. Hollywood, Florida: Al-Baz Publishing, Inc., 1997.